D1712579

EDGE BOOKS

DOGS ON THE JOB

SEARCH AND RESCUE DOGS

by Gail Langer Karwoski

Consultant:
Gary Garrison
North American Police Work Dog Association

CAPSTONE PRESS
a capstone imprint

Edge Books are published by Capstone Press,
1710 Roe Crest Drive, North Mankato, Minnesota 56003
www.capstonepub.com

Library of Congress Cataloging-in-Publication Data
Karwoski, Gail, 1949-
Search and rescue dogs / by Gail Langer Karwoski.
pages cm—(Edge books. Dogs on the job)
Includes index.
ISBN 978-1-4765-0131-4 (library binding)
ISBN 978-1-4765-3387-2 (ebook PDF)
1. Search dogs—Juvenile literature. 2. Rescue dogs—Juvenile literature.
I. Title.
SF428.73.K37 2014
636.7'0886—dc23   2012051697

Editorial Credits
Brenda Haugen, editor; Kyle Grenz, designer; Marcie Spence, media researcher;
Laura Manthe, production specialist

Photo Credits
Alamy Images: ZUMA Wire Service, 14; AP Images: Alan Diaz, File, 18, Dave Martin,
cover, Ed Bailey, 28; Getty Images: Andrea Booher/FEMA, 5, George Best, 4, Mai/
Time Life Pictures, 24-25, Marcos Townsend/AFP, 17, Nicholas Kamm/AFP, 22,
Universal History Archive, 11; iStockphoto: wpohldesign, 12; Newscom: Brian Cahn/
ZUMA Press, 15, CB2/ZOB/WENN, 19, ColorChinaPhotos/ZUMA Press, 20, Gloria
Ferniz/ZUMA Press, 13, Thomas Yau/EPN, 29, Xinhau/ZUMA Press, 9; Shutterstock:
amidala76, 8, 23, Jim Parkin, 6, 7, Magati, 10, Peter Baxter, 16, Susan DeLoach, 27

Printed in the United States of America in Stevens Point, Wisconsin.
032013   007227WZF13

Table of Contents

CHAPTER 1

Four-Legged Heroes

Peter Davis and his dog Appollo started searching for survivors 15 minutes after terrorists crashed planes into New York's World Trade Center on September 11, 2001. They were the first Search and Rescue (SAR) dog team to arrive at the scene.

Peter Davis and Appollo were members of the K-9 unit of the New York City Police Department. Appollo died in 2006.

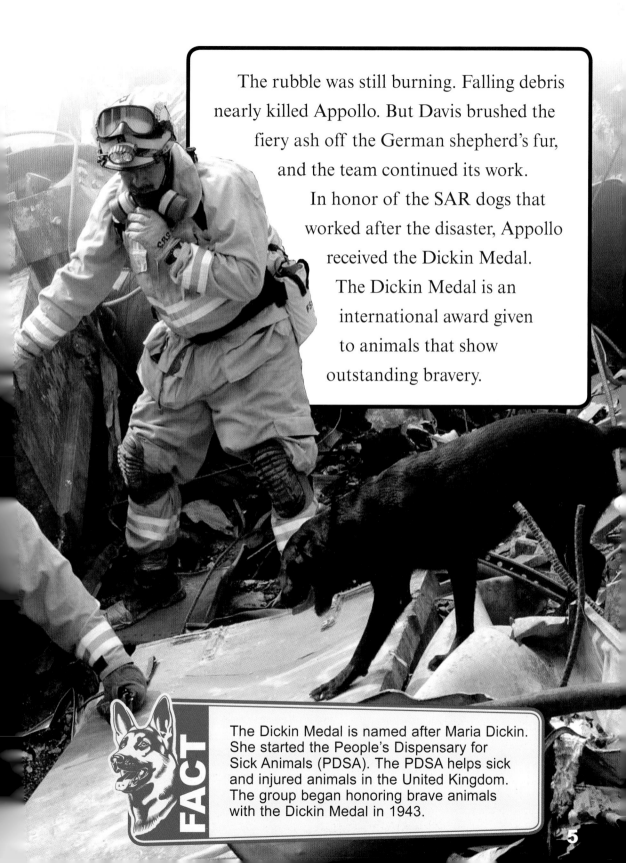

The rubble was still burning. Falling debris nearly killed Appollo. But Davis brushed the fiery ash off the German shepherd's fur, and the team continued its work.

In honor of the SAR dogs that worked after the disaster, Appollo received the Dickin Medal. The Dickin Medal is an international award given to animals that show outstanding bravery.

FACT

The Dickin Medal is named after Maria Dickin. She started the People's Dispensary for Sick Animals (PDSA). The PDSA helps sick and injured animals in the United Kingdom. The group began honoring brave animals with the Dickin Medal in 1943.

In an emergency, every moment counts. SAR dogs can cover an area faster and better than people can. Without SAR dogs, rescuers might arrive too late to save an injured victim or a lost child.

SAR dogs are trained to follow their noses. Some dogs track a person's path or follow a trail from a known starting point. They may sniff the belongings of the missing person and try to pick up that scent along the trail.

Smelling People

How does a dog detect human scent? People shed rafts of dead skin. Rafts are made of dead cells. Bacteria digest these cells and give off gas that a dog can smell. Rafts are carried by air, pass through small cracks in rubble, and rise to the surface of water. As air moves, the scent flows downwind and spreads out. An SAR dog keeps its nose in the air and sniffs. When it detects a human scent, it heads in the direction where the scent is strongest.

SAR dogs can search for the scent of any victim, alive or dead. SAR dogs can even find victims who have been covered by ash, soil, snow, or water.

FACT

A human nose has about 5 million cells devoted to smell, but a dog has up to 200 million.

raft—a flake of dead skin cells

cell—the smallest unit of a living thing

Each SAR dog is trained to work in certain settings, such as wooded areas or in cities. Some dogs search for victims of avalanches. Others are trained to look for people after disasters, such as hurricanes. Sometimes an SAR dog is cross-trained to work in more than one setting.

FACT

A dog can sometimes smell a body that has been buried under soil for decades.

avalanche—a large mass of ice, snow, or earth that suddenly moves down the side of a mountain

Search and rescue requires teamwork. The dogs can detect scents people can't smell. Dogs can crawl into spaces where people can't fit. They also see better at night than people can. Meanwhile, the dogs' handlers interpret their dogs' signals. Handlers often map out search areas as well.

CHAPTER 2

A History of Helping

Dogs first rescued people in the late 1700s in the Great St. Bernard Pass in the Alps mountain range in Switzerland. A St. Bernard named Barry was one of the first SAR dogs. He found people buried by avalanches. During his lifetime, Barry saved more than 40 people. In his most famous rescue, Barry found a small boy in an ice **cavern** and brought him to safety.

St. Bernards are friendly, gentle dogs.

cavern—a deep hollow place underground

The SAR dogs in the Swiss Alps were owned by monks. The animals worked in pairs. After an avalanche, the dogs searched for victims. They could smell people trapped under the snow and would dig them out. While one dog warmed the survivor with its body heat, the other dog ran to **alert** the monks.

In the 1900s, SAR dogs also helped people during times of war. During the two world wars, SAR dogs were used in Europe. They searched for people trapped under bombed buildings.

FACT

St. Bernards are strong dogs that can weigh as much as 200 pounds (91 kilograms).

alert—to bring something to a person's attention; also a behavior to get a person's attention

    SAR dogs have
a long history in
the United States
as well as Europe.
Bill and Jean
Syrotuck formed the
American Rescue Dog
Association (ARDA) in
1972. ARDA is a national
organization for German
shepherd owners who train
their dogs in SAR.

A dog handled by Jean Syrotuck rescued a person after an avalanche on Washington's Mount Rainier in 1969. This was the first use of an avalanche dog in the United States.

The group created standards to certify dogs and handlers. ARDA also developed the sector search method for SAR teams. During a sector search, a search area is divided into sections. Each section is assigned to an SAR dog and handler. Today there are several SAR dog organizations in the United States. These groups include a variety of purebred dog breeds, as well as mixed-breed dogs.

certify—to officially recognize the training, skills, and abilities of a person or dog

sector—a smaller part of a larger area

purebred—having parents of the same breed

In time, more advanced training was created for SAR dogs. After a political extremist bombed the Federal Building in Oklahoma City in 1995, there was a lot of rubble to search. At the time, just 15 SAR dog teams in the United States had advanced training to deal with disasters such as bombings. Wilma Melville and her black lab, Murphy, had that advanced training. At the bombing site, Melville listened for Murphy's bark. The bark was Murphy's signal that he had found a person.

Wilma Melville

Melville knew more dogs were needed to help in such disasters. She decided to do something about the problem. Since firefighters are usually the first rescuers at a disaster scene, she created a group that donates SAR dogs to firefighters. It is called the National Disaster Search Dog Foundation. Through donations, the group covers the training costs of SAR dogs and gives them to firefighters free of cost. The dogs are chosen from shelters and other places that rescue animals.

FACT

It takes up to five years and costs up to $15,000 to train a disaster dog.

CHAPTER 3

The Best Dogs for the Job

The larger working dog breeds are best known for search and rescue work. German shepherds are often used by police. Newfoundlands are often trained for water rescues. Bloodhounds are mainly used for ground tracking. But many trainers think that an SAR dog's breed is not as important as its personality. A trainer looks for a young dog that shows no signs of aggression or fear around crowds, loud noises, and strange places. An SAR dog must be social around people.

aggression—fierce or threatening behavior

An Inspiring Dog

The Federal Emergency Management Agency (FEMA) certifies dogs for disaster searches. Sage, a border collie, was a FEMA disaster dog. On her first assignment, Sage was sent to the Pentagon after the terrorist attack on September 11, 2001. Sage found the remains of one of the attackers. Sage also worked after hurricanes Katrina and Rita struck the Gulf Coast in 2005.

Sage was diagnosed with lung cancer in 2009. Her handler, Dianne Whetsel, brought Sage to camps for children with cancer. Sage inspired the kids. The American Humane Association honored Sage in 2011 for her SAR work.

An SAR dog also must have a strong "play and prey" drive. To a dog, searching is a game. A dog that never tires of finding a toy may be a great candidate for search and rescue work. A very active dog may not make an ideal pet for many families, so these dogs often end up in shelters. But high energy is a good trait for an SAR dog.

Search and rescue teams work at the World Trade Center in New York in 2001.

trait—a quality or characteristic that makes one person or animal different from another

17

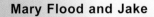

A black lab named Jake was a rescued dog who became a rescuer. When Mary Flood found Jake in a shelter, he was a 10-month-old puppy. He had a broken leg and a damaged hip. After surgery to fix his injuries, one of his rear legs was 2 inches (5 centimeters) shorter than the other. But his disability never slowed him down.

Flood trained Jake as an SAR dog. Jake became a FEMA-certified disaster dog. He searched for victims after the 9/11 World Trade Center attack and after hurricanes Katrina and Rita.

Preparing a dog for search and rescue begins with obedience training. Dogs learn several commands, such as sit, stay, and heel. SAR dogs also are taught to stop instantly and to back up. During some searches, dogs will not be able to hear their handlers' voices, so they may be trained to respond to hand signals too.

SAR dogs practice their footing on all kinds of surfaces. They may have to do searches on ice, in holes, or in wooded areas. They may work in unstable buildings or in rubble.

SAR dogs learn to ride in various vehicles. During searches, they may have to ride in noisy helicopters or boats. Dogs that are afraid of riding in these vehicles may not make good SAR dogs.

obedience—obeying rules and commands

heel—a command telling a dog to walk by a handler's left heel

19

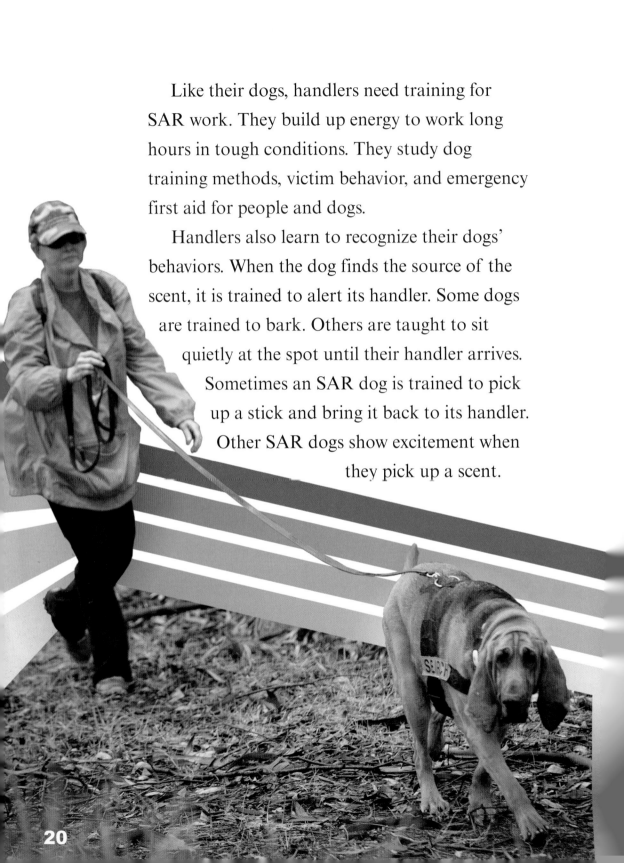

Like their dogs, handlers need training for SAR work. They build up energy to work long hours in tough conditions. They study dog training methods, victim behavior, and emergency first aid for people and dogs.

Handlers also learn to recognize their dogs' behaviors. When the dog finds the source of the scent, it is trained to alert its handler. Some dogs are trained to bark. Others are taught to sit quietly at the spot until their handler arrives. Sometimes an SAR dog is trained to pick up a stick and bring it back to its handler. Other SAR dogs show excitement when they pick up a scent.

Before SAR teams are sent on missions, they must pass tests to prove their readiness. Several organizations for SAR dogs offer both training clinics and certification. Among these groups is the Search and Rescue Dogs of the United States.

CHAPTER 4

Heroes in Action

An SAR dog team must be ready whenever an emergency happens. Sometimes a handler must drive for hours to reach the site of the emergency. During a national or international disaster, an SAR team may fly to the scene.

SAR teams arrive in Japan to search for earthquake victims in 2011.

Most survivors are found in the first day of searching. Rescuers call this period the "golden 24 hours."

A search may take an hour, or it may take a week or longer. As soon as an SAR team arrives, it may be asked to do a quick search before a more thorough search is organized.

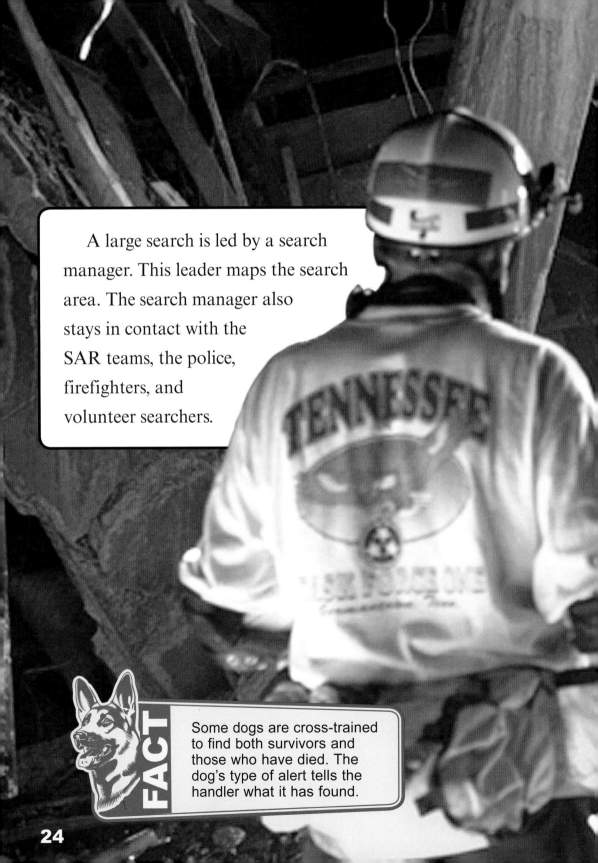

A large search is led by a search manager. This leader maps the search area. The search manager also stays in contact with the SAR teams, the police, firefighters, and volunteer searchers.

FACT

Some dogs are cross-trained to find both survivors and those who have died. The dog's type of alert tells the handler what it has found.

The search manager assigns each SAR team to an area and to a work shift. This prevents problems such as missing an area or searching a place more than once. Working long hours can make a dog or handler overly tired. By limiting the time a team works, mistakes are less likely.

shift—a set amount of time to work

When a search dog behaves like it may have found a person, a second dog may be brought to the site. If the second dog has the same reaction, rescuers will focus on this area. At the site of a large disaster, handlers often mark spots where dogs showed interest. The handlers note the spots with brightly colored tape or paint and then move on to find other victims. Rescuers follow right behind the dog teams to begin the work of digging out victims.

SAR dogs practice walking on seesaws. This teaches them how to balance themselves on rubble and other surfaces that may move.

An SAR dog must stay focused at a scene. It ignores the scents of other searchers at the scene. It also ignores loud noises, machines that rumble, and rubble that moves underfoot. It also must ignore the tempting smells of food.

SAR dogs and their handlers face dangerous situations to save others. An earthquake struck San Salvador, the capital of El Salvador, in 1986. SAR dog Aly and his handler, Caroline Hebard, were sent to help by the U.S. government. As Hebard and the German shepherd searched beneath a collapsed hotel, an aftershock destroyed their escape route. Suddenly the rescuers were in need of rescue! Aly bounded into the darkness. When Aly reappeared, Hebard and others who were trapped followed the dog through a narrow passage to safety.

Caroline Hebard and Aly

Search and rescue work requires many hours of training. The dogs and their handlers form lifelong partnerships. After the dogs retire, they often remain important members of their handlers' families. SAR dogs were chosen in part because of their close bonds with people. In their old age, these dogs enjoy relaxing with their beloved human companions.

aftershock—a small earthquake that follows a larger one

Glossary

aftershock (AF-tur-shok)—a small earthquake that follows a larger one

aggression (uh-GREH-shuhn)—fierce or threatening behavior

alert (uh-LURT)—to bring something to a person's attention; also a behavior to get a person's attention

avalanche (A-vuh-lanch)—a large mass of ice, snow, or earth that suddenly moves down the side of a mountain

cavern (KA-vuhrn)—a deep hollow place underground

cell (SEL)—the smallest unit of a living thing

certify (SUHR-tuh-fye)—to officially recognize the training, skills, and abilities of a person or dog

heel (HEEL)—a command telling a dog to walk by a handler's left heel

obedience (oh-BEE-dee-uhnss)—obeying rules and commands

purebred (PYOOR-bred)—having parents of the same breed

raft (RAHFT)—a flake of dead skin cells

sector (SEK-tur)—a smaller part of a larger area

shift (SHIFT)—a set amount of time to work

trait (TRAYT)—a quality or characteristic that makes one person or animal different from another

Read More

Bozzo, Linda. *Search and Rescue Dog Heroes.*
Amazing Working Dogs. Berkeley Heights, N.J.: Bailey
Books/Enslow, 2011.

Gagne, Tammy. *German Shepherds.* All About Dogs.
Mankato, Minn.: Capstone Press, 2009.

Goldish, Meish. *Ground Zero Dogs.* Dog Heroes.
New York: Bearport Pub., 2013.

Internet Sites

FactHound offers a safe, fun way to find Internet sites
related to this book. All of the sites on FactHound have
been researched by our staff.

Here's all you do:

Visit *www.facthound.com*

Type in this code: 9781476501314

 Check out projects, games and lots more at
www.capstonekids.com

Index